coordination. Many positions in defense agencies are filled by men from private business whose terms are short and indefinite. The maximum salary for a government officer, other than a Cabinet member, is now $14,800 yearly. Prevailing salaries in private business are so much higher as to prevent government obtaining a fair share of scarce executive talent.

Mr. Corson's suggestions are pointed. They are deduced from a keen analysis of present sore spots. His program for immediate action is reprinted on the back of the jacket. For the long run, Mr. Corson makes clear the necessity for: (1) creating an awareness of the critical need for a larger supply of executives and potential executives in the Federal government (2) inducing a larger proportion of each year's crop of the ablest college graduates to enter government service (3) raising the maximum salary to at least $25,000 and (4) offering other incentives such as leaves of absence, assurance of proper education for the children of government employees and (5) creating a pool of career administrators and a complementary "public service reserve" to provide a mobile and expansible supply of qualified executive talent.

About the author

Mr. Corson is well qualified by experience as an executive in the Federal government and in private business to write this book. Now a management consultant in the firm of McKinsey and Company, Washington, D. C., he has been, in succession, director of the Bureau of Old Age and Survivors Insurance of the Social Security Board, director of the United States Employment S[illegible] [illegible]puty general of UNRRA in charge [illegible]ation, and assistant business [illegible] the Washington *Post*. He pre[illegible] report at the request of the [illegible]rporation.

EXECUTIVES *for the* FEDERAL SERVICE

EXECUTIVES *for the* FEDERAL SERVICE

A PROGRAM FOR ACTION IN TIME OF CRISIS

by JOHN J. CORSON

New York 1952
COLUMBIA UNIVERSITY PRESS

PUBLISHED IN GREAT BRITAIN, CANADA, AND INDIA
BY GEOFFREY CUMBERLEGE, OXFORD UNIVERSITY PRESS,
LONDON, TORONTO, AND BOMBAY

MANUFACTURED IN THE UNITED STATES OF AMERICA

THIS book was made possible in part by funds granted by the Carnegie Corporation of New York and was prepared under the auspices of Public Administration Clearing House. Neither the Carnegie Corporation nor Public Administration Clearing House is, however, the author, owner, publisher, or proprietor of this publication, and neither is to be understood as approving any of the statements made or views expressed therein.

PREFACE

IN each of two world wars the United States government has brought in executives from private life to head its emergency programs. These men—some of them dollar-a-year men, others serving under other types of appointment—have generally enlisted for the duration and have been eager to get back to their regular occupations with the return of peace.

This system, while disorderly enough at best, worked reasonably well when it was possible to assume that each war would soon be followed by a relatively long period of genuine peace. When the crisis is not profound enough to demand unreserved sacrifice by private citizens and private corporations alike, however, the problem is a more difficult one. While the man with business experience is essential in some types of federal operations, the minuteman or short-term volunteer is often no better prepared to enlist and serve in the complex area of federal administration during the long cold war than the untrained militiaman was suited for the difficult techniques of modern combat.

The crisis in our international affairs, and the resulting

problems of economic control and industrial mobilization, have shown up the weaknesses of our civilian executive machinery. But the weaknesses had been there all the while. Several decades ago the United States tackled the job of reforming the spoils system, but only halfheartedly; it passed laws and set up machinery to put the great mass of government employees on a civil service basis, but it provided nothing like a real career system for the top-ranking civilian government executive. As a result, the civilian side of the Federal government is weak by comparison with the miltary side—and this lack of balance may in the long run have grave effects on the nature of public policy.

In short, as a nation we have had so much faith in constitutional arrangements and legal reforms that we have not bothered to provide our Government with a career system that would bring into its top executive positions a large enough share of the nation's best executive and administrative talents. Whether we can now do so is a test of our ability as a free nation to govern ourselves responsibly and efficiently.

The crucial nature of this emergency problem, and its long-range significance in the American governmental system, led the Carnegie Corporation to initiate a study of *Executives for the Federal Service* early in 1951. The Corporation requested Public Administration Clearing House to undertake such a study and the Clearing House in turn requested Mr. John J. Corson to work with the Federal officials concerned and to prepare the report.

Mr. Corson, who is now the head of the Washington

office of the firm of McKinsey & Company, Management Consultants, was eminently qualified for this task. He has been, in succession, Director of the Bureau of Old Age and Survivors Insurance of the Social Security Board, Director of the United States Employment Service, Deputy Director General of UNRRA in charge of administration, and an executive of *The Washington Post.*

The circulation of Mr. Corson's report to a limited number of executives in the Federal service and in private business aroused so much interest that the Carnegie Corporation and Public Administration Clearing House were glad to make possible its publication.

The problem of improving the executive personnel of the public service is a difficult one. Doubtless no single report could provide a perfect prescription for action by the Federal government. But Mr. Corson has described and illuminated one of the important problems that American society must face in the mid-twentieth century.

HERBERT EMMERICH

Chicago, Illinois
February 15, 1952

CONTENTS

EXECUTIVES *for the* FEDERAL SERVICE

I. THE EXECUTIVE CRISIS

IN a real sense, the destiny of the democratic idea rests on the government of the United States. Circumstance has made this country the leader of that portion of the world that places its faith in the worth and capacity of the individual. Our success in discharging this unprecedented responsibility rests in principal part on the capacity of the Federal government to provide leadership to the American people at home, and through their governments to the democratic peoples of the world.

The Korean crisis made clear and immediate the measure of this responsibility. To meet it, the Federal government tooled up to perform new functions. Together, these functions promise to provide the material needs for the defense of the free world at a minimal and equitably distributed cost to all citizens. The achievement of these objectives depends upon the capacity of the Federal government, and especially upon those men and women who occupy its top-level positions.

But the governmental institutions responsible for the

mobilization of the American economy for defense suffer from the lack of direction which typifies a new institution directed by men and women unfamiliar with a little-traveled field. The essential ingredient for the successful discharge of the vast responsibilities that have been assumed—human leadership for each of a score of emergency governmental agencies, offices, and bureaus—is distressingly scarce.[1]

For an indefinite period this nation must remain constantly mobilized. Can the mobilization activities made essential by the world crisis—the production of materiel, the control of prices and wages, and the provision for civilian defense in the event of attack—be planned and administered indefinitely by a half staff, available for from three to twelve months into the future or devoting only part time to the public business? The governmental leadership must be equal to the task of applying such controls as may be essential in full recognition of the vital necessity of keeping the American economy healthy, alert, and enterprising; the current struggle for the preservation of freedom will be determined more by the capacity of the American economy to produce and to grow than by the capacity of our fighting forces. The dynamic and enterprising economy that is needed to outproduce the Communist nations requires "(1) rapid progress in technology; (2) adventurous and imaginative business-

[1] In a speech before the American Institute of Electrical Engineers, January 22, 1951, Karl T. Compton, Chairman of the Board of the Massachusetts Institute of Technology, declared that a shortage of trained leaders for key posts "is the most serious bottleneck in the nation's defense program."

men . . . and (3) investors who are willing to take long chances in the hope of making big gains." [2] Hence, emergency agencies must be directed with a sensitive appreciation of the necessity of stimulating business initiative while applying the controls that at the moment are required.

Yet this demand for executive leadership is but the immediate aspect of an old and critical problem of democratic government. President Truman has testified, on a number of occasions, to the difficulties he has encountered in obtaining competent men for top-level Federal jobs. At the Princeton Bicentennial celebration he suggested that the "government must bring into service from business and labor and the professions the best qualified persons to fill posts at all levels" while taking "several steps to make the career service more attractive to the kind of men and women it needs." [3]

James V. Forrestal, one-time Secretary of the Navy and later Secretary of Defense, spoke out on several oc-

[2] Sumner Slichter, *What's Ahead for American Business?* (Little Brown & Co., 1951), p. 29.

[3] See the President's comments at press conferences as reported in *The New York Times* on October 21, 1949, and December 4, 1949. On October 21, 1949, the President, in commenting on the refusal of the Senate to confirm Leland Olds for reappointment to the Federal Power Commission deplored the difficulties of finding qualified men for public office because of what he called the slanderous treatment by members of Congress and gossip columnists which they suffer while in office. On December 3, 1949, *The New York Times* reported that "Three factors, age and fatigue, the economic lure of outside employment, and the hazards of public life, have been making it increasingly difficult for President Truman to keep together his essential high policy staff." This report was founded on the President's difficulty at that time in filling the posts of Chairman, Atomic Energy Commission; Chairman, National Security Resources Board; and Counsel to the President.

casions during the years preceding his unfortunate death in 1949. He lamented the government's inability to induce an adequate number of the nation's ablest minds to enter the highly important business of government.[4] William L. Batt, former vice-chairman of the War Production Board and President of SKF Industries, Inc., proposed in 1946 "that for men who have qualities that particularly adapt them for public service their companies should consider anticipating the normal retirement date to allow such men to go into policy-making Government posts while they have the strength of mind and body to give something of real value."[5] And Secretary of the Army Royall in January, 1948, spoke of the unwillingness of top business executives to serve at prevailing government salaries; he urged business, labor, and farm organizations to lend their "most promising young executives to the government to fill most important administrative posts."[6]

Yet now, when another emergency necessitates the recruitment of competent men and women for the civilian as well as the military establishment of the Federal government, essential top-level personnel are lacking.

Ten or more individuals declined the President's invitation to serve as Economic Stabilization Administrator before an acceptance was obtained. Before a Director of the Office of Price Stabilization could be obtained, thirty individuals were offered the position. Some defense posts

[4] "If the U.S. Is Really to Do a Job"—an article in *The New York Times Magazine*, May 9, 1948.

[5] A speech before the American Management Association meeting at the Waldorf Astoria Hotel, New York City.

[6] A speech before the Boston Chamber of Commerce, January 30, 1948.

in the departments of Defense, Interior, State, and Commerce have gone begging for months. In the emergency agencies numerous positions have been filled by executives serving (a) on a part-time basis, (b) for a definitely limited tenure, i.e., ninety days, six months, or one year, or (c) "without compensation" while continuing on the payroll of a private employer.

Such agencies as the Office of Price Stabilization, the National Production Authority, the Defense Transport Administration, the Defense Electric Power Administration, and the Defense Production Administration have been given loosely drafted assignments of major importance and expected to discharge them without adequate staff, space, or facilities. The permanent personnel agencies of the Federal government provide a reasonably adequate supply of clerical and stenographic help but are of little assistance in procuring executives. Many executive jobs are filled not by the ablest of the career civil servants but by the "opportunists" and "drifters" from among them. A minority of the executive positions are filled by businessmen who serve during the emergency without compensation. Their effectiveness is reduced by their unfamiliarity with government and they are frequently assigned to positions in which their impartiality is challenged. The inevitable result is that these agencies discharge functions affecting the lives and businesses of millions in an aura of confusion, haste, and amateurish zeal.

THE FOCAL QUESTIONS

The present executive crisis forces us to face up to five focal questions.

1. For what types of positions are executives needed and what talents are required?

2. How does the government go about the selection of executives, and are its methods equal to the task?

3. Why do individuals refuse important, influential, and prestigious positions tendered them? What characteristics of executive positions in the Federal government cause competent and trained executives from outside the public service to decline opportunities to serve?

4. What can be done to obtain the executive talent that is needed for the immediate emergency? Is it possible to meet this emergency, as the United States has met other emergencies, on a "minuteman" basis?

5. Are there ways of developing within the Federal service a more adequate and more respected corps of executives to man the Federal establishments and to provide administrative leadership in times of emergency?

There are steps which can be taken immediately to make available the top-level executives that are needed. These steps must be taken promptly. But steps that will suffice only for the current emergency are not enough. The crisis this nation faces appears to be of indefinite duration. A more permanent solution to the need for competent executives is essential. That solution will not be found until there is developed a public awareness of the need for able executives in the public service. To create that awareness is a task demanding the ingenuity that can combat both the impression left in the public mind by the "pastel mink scandal" and the inherited disrespect that Americans have for those in public employment. Yet that public awareness and greater appreciation of the public service must be created.

On such public understanding can be built a program (1) to bring a larger proportion of the ablest youth into the public service each year; (2) to retain and develop these men and women until they can serve in the most important top-level Federal positions; (3) to identify potential executives; (4) to establish the principles upon which a career in public management can be founded; and finally (5) to create a reservoir of manpower which will include the executive talent needed for a dynamic democratic government.

These tasks—the creation of public awareness of this critical need and the design of both emergency and long-run programs to provide essential executive talent for the Federal government—deserves painstaking consideration and widespread public attention. Not since 1934 has the problem of public service personnel received thoroughgoing attention. In the meantime the role of the Federal government has vastly expanded. In the 1950's the Federal government must attain a garrison state while nurturing the liberties and initiative which flourish only among a democratic people. The need is to demonstrate the human requirements of this expanded government and to give new vigor and positive direction to the whole civil service movement. Simultaneously there is an urgent need to make meaningful to the American people the new role of the Federal government of the United States in the 1950's, when this country provides for its people an increasingly broad range of public services and for the world the leadership and much of the resources that preserve the democratic idea.

The comments that follow are designed, first, to describe steps which may be immediately helpful in meeting the problem of obtaining executives for those governmental activities which have been established to meet the existing emergency and, second, to suggest ways and means of developing, in the long run, a more adequate corps of executives within the Federal service. The suggestions that are made and the answers that are given to the questions listed above have been distilled from interviews with a large number of government administrators, recruitment and personnel officials, members of Congress, newspaper men and radio commentators, and businessmen both within and without the Federal service. These suggestions do not constitute a definitive answer to either the emergency problem or to the more basic long-run problem of manning an expanding central government. They should stimulate needed action and even more urgently needed public recognition of the fact that the public business must be managed with all the skill and capacity it requires.

II. THE DEMAND FOR EXECUTIVES

THE NUMBER

THE management of the executive branch of the Federal government required approximately 3,300 executives in 1950.[1] This number includes only those who manage and direct the activities of Federal agencies.[2] It does not include scientists and professional people—actuaries, chemists, doctors, engineers, lawyers, physicists, and others—unless they simultaneously manage and direct an organizational unit. It does not include uniformed members of the armed services or members of the Foreign Service. Roughly, it includes those individuals serving the Federal government as civilian executives at salaries of $10,000 per annum and above. This group constitutes but a handful of the more than two and a quarter million

[1] As of June 30, 1950, the Civil Service Commission reported a total of 2,306 individuals in positions classified in grade GS-15. To this total must be added 650 positions now classified in the "super grades" GS-16-18 and a total of approximately 400 unclassified executive positions as directors, commissioners, etc.

[2] Milton Mandell of the U.S. Civil Service Commission, in an unpublished study of the problem of executive selection, defines an executive as "one whose job requires that he spend at least 50 percent of his time in program planning, program selling, and coordination."

Federal civilian employees. The total salaries paid to this group of key officials makes up less than 2 percent of the wages and salaries paid to all employees.

THEIR INFLUENCE

Yet this small group determines the caliber of our national defense effort, of the administration of justice, of the conservation of natural resources, of welfare services, of the management of our foreign affairs, and of the various other services the national government performs. Given imaginative, enterprising, capable, and industrious men and women in these posts, the interest, zeal, enthusiasm, and efficiency of all Federal employees are materially enhanced. Given slothful, dull, untrained, self-seeking or precedent-following individuals in these posts, the productivity and enterprise of the great body of Federal employees are decreased. Upon the shoulders of these men and women rests the responsibility for planning the activities, stimulating the interest, reviewing the work, and insuring the efficiency of the large and growing number of employees on the rolls of the Federal government.[3]

[3] "The responsibilities of management in the various departments of the executive branch are today so great that danger to the welfare and security of the country, as well as immense financial losses, can result from incompetence on the top-executive level. High caliber executives can eliminate cumbersome and wasteful forms of management." The Commission on Organization of the Executive Branch of the Government, Personnel Management (February 1949).

See also House of Representatives, 81st Congress, 2nd Session, Report 2457, Part VI, p. 145: "It is universally agreed that agency management holds the key to optimum employee utilization. Although the management of a large Government enterprise presents many complex problems, most of them center upon the expenditure of funds and/or the assignment of people. The goal of management would appear to

TALENTS REQUIRED

A mere listing of the titles of key executive jobs would illustrate the wide range of fields into which the services of the Federal government reach and, as a consequence, the wide assortment of competences demanded of this group of executives. Moreover, neither the number nor the variety of competences required is ever static. Within the past two decades the Federal government has grown from a relatively small establishment including a total of 600,000 employees to a present total of 2,250,000 employees. As the Federal establishment has grown, the number of executives, too, has grown. This number has been expanded further by the persistent undertaking by the Federal government of more and more functions.

Consider, for example, five agencies of the Federal government established within these two decades. These agencies are the Social Security Administration, the National Labor Relations Board, the Rural Electrification Administration, the Atomic Energy Commission, and the Economic Cooperation Administration (now the Mutual Security Agency). These five agencies need executives expert in social insurance, labor relations, power generation and distribution, foreign trade, international affairs, and nuclear physics. In addition, these agencies require, for the management of their various departments, actuaries, specialists in machine accounting, economists, lawyers, electrical engineers, purchasing agents, journal-

be the optimum use of these resources—monetary and human—within fixed maximum limits of dollars and employees."

ists, town managers, chemists, and experts in budgeting, accounting, and personnel administration.

These specialists must possess still other talents to succeed as governmental executives. They must be capable of formulating policies which will govern a whole industry or the entire nation. Their concern is comprehensive; it is not focused on a single enterprise. They must be capable, too, of interpreting and reinterpreting their plans and policies constantly to the Congress and its committees, to such control agencies as the Bureau of the Budget and the General Accounting Office, to the spokesmen for pressure groups, the representatives of the press and other media of communication, and to the public.[4] They must be capable of operating effectively within the arena of politics, for they are the agents of and are accountable to a democratic, representative government. For these tasks they must be capable of popular leadership. They must be able simultaneously to coordinate and manage the work of numerous organizational units for which they are responsible. This ability will include the vision and skill that will enable them to stimulate the minds and liberate the energies of the individuals that make up these organizational units.

The public executive, in contrast to the private execu-

[4] Dr. Alan Valentine, first administrator of the Economic Stabilization Administration, declared in his first public statement after resigning from this post that an officeholder has to curry favor with organized labor, the Democratic National Committee, and the White House secretariat. One wonders whether he was criticizing an objectionable "undercover government," as he described it, or whether he was picturing the environment within which most major officials succeed or fail.

tive, must possess still three other qualities. He must be able to think in terms of public policy and to anticipate the effects of a governmental action in a thousand different places. He also must have an "ingrained disposition to put the public interest first." Finally, he must have a sense of public relations or a political sense. This involves a willingness to be exposed to citizen reaction and an ability to anticipate reactions and to adjust administrative programs promptly.[5]

SUMMARY OF DEMAND

Each year approximately ten percent of the executive positions in the Federal government are vacated by death, retirement, or resignation.[6] This is the annual and inexorable need for permanent executive talent. But there is an additional substantial and recurring need for executives. Within the lifetime of this generation there have been four emergencies—World War I, the depression period of 1931–37, World War II, and now the Cold War of the 1950's. Each emergency has called for the establishment of new and temporary agencies of the

[5] See Paul H. Appleby, *Big Democracy* (New York: Alfred A. Knopf, 1945), pp. 39–43, for a description of the important qualifications of a governmental executive.

[6] House of Representatives, 81st Congress, 2nd Session, Report 2457, Part VI, "Investigation of Employee Utilization in the Executive Department and Agencies," indicates the results of a study of employee turnover by classified grade in four agencies of the Federal government during the fiscal year 1950—the Federal Security Agency, Treasury Department, Interior Department, and General Services Administration. In these agencies the annual turnover among employees in Grade 15 and above was 10.7. Assuming this rate to be typical of the turnover in other departments, the annual number of executive positions to be filled would approximate 350.

Federal government—e.g., the War Industries Board of 1916, the National Recovery Administration (NRA) and the Works Progress Administration (WPA) of the depression 1930's, the War Production Board and the Office of Price Administration of World War II, and now the Federal Civil Defense Administration, the Economic Stabilization Administration, and the National Production Authority of the 1950's. These and other agencies were established to perform functions and to exercise over the lives and businesses of the American people controls which previously had not been the concern of the Federal government. The activities to be planned and directed involved, in many instances, tasks with which the permanent corps of executives within the Federal government were not versed. The effective performance of some tasks required a familiarity with industrial technology, the competitive status of firms within the industry, and the personalities in key industrial positions. Hence, the Federal government has sought in each emergency many executives from private business, from academic institutions, and from labor organizations to launch these critically important agencies.

The current emergency has focused attention on the great difficulties that the Federal government encounters in obtaining experienced executives to direct these emergency agencies. Simultaneously, the permanent establishments of the Federal government are called upon to asume additional functions. They, too, seek additional executives. The demand for executives is great. The supply of competent executives is small. There are few individuals with the capacity to plan and manage large affairs, with a keen understanding of the importance of initiative in a free-enterprise economy and of how such initiative may be nurtured, with the temperament suitable for service within government, and with a desire to recognize and to serve the public interest.

III. FINDING AND HIRING EXECUTIVES

HOW does the government go about finding and hiring executives? Is there an established organizational machinery which seeks out competent individuals with the particular skills needed for those who head the Federal departments and emergency establishments? Out of the experience of recent decades and of previous emergencies within the current generation, have lessons been learned which make the task simpler?

THE PRESIDENT RECRUITS

Consider the selection of individuals to serve as under secretaries, assistant secretaries, and solicitors of the twelve executive departments. There are a total of sixty-eight positions of this rank. More than 50 percent of the incumbents of these positions are men who had occupied previous positions within the Federal government and were promoted to the positions they now occupy. Approximately one third of all these positions are filled by political appointees. The balance, approximately one sixth of the total, owe their appointment to a previous personal acquaintanceship or association with the head of the department.

Technically, the incumbents of most of these positions are appointed by the President "with the advice and consent of the Senate." Actually, however, the President appoints to these positions the individuals whom the members of his Cabinet select. In a minority of instances this means that the Secretary of a department nominates an individual with whom he has been associated in private life (as, for example, the Under Secretary of the Department of Labor), or an individual with whom he was associated in previous government service (as General Marshall was associated with his Under Secretary of Defense, Mr. Lovett). More often the Secretary nominates an individual with whom he has worked, whose work he has observed, and in whose abilities he has confidence. This factor of personal acquaintanceship is a decisive one in the selection of this group of executives.[1]

The President, in addition, must appoint the members or heads of such agencies as: the Atomic Energy Com-

[1] Chester Barnard, *The Functions of an Executive* (Cambridge, Harvard University Press, 1938), p. 223, says: "In all the good organizations I have observed . . . informal organizations operate. . . . The general method of maintaining an informal executive organization is so to operate and to select and promote executives that a general condition of compatibility of personnel is maintained. Perhaps often and certainly occasionally men cannot be promoted or selected, or even must be relieved, because they cannot function, because they 'do not fit,' where there is no question of formal competence. This question of 'fitness' involves such matters as education, experience, age, sex, personal distinctions, prestige, race, nationality, faith, politics, sectional antecedents; and such very specific personal traits as manners, speech, personal appearance, etc."

mission, the Mutual Security Agency, the Federal Communications Commission, the Federal Mediation and Conciliation Service, the Board of Governors of the Federal Reserve System, the Federal Security Agency, the Interstate Commerce Commission, the Reconstruction Finance Corporation, the Tennessee Valley Authority, the U.S. Civil Service Commission, and the Veterans Administration.

The selection of top-level personnel for these and many other agencies is made the more difficult by the fact that there is no Cabinet member to nominate appointees and by the strong pressures of those groups which have special concern in appointments. For example, both employer and labor organizations are concerned with appointments to the National Labor Relations Board, the Federal Mediation and Conciliation Service, and the Railroad Retirement Board. The organized veterans are concerned with the appointment of an administrator of the Veterans Administration.

To aid him in the selection of competent executives, the President has an Administrative Assistant specializing in personnel matters. In practice the President frequently relies upon the Chairman of the Commission on which a vacancy arises to suggest an appointee. Yet despite the aid of his Administrative Assistant and of the heads of independent agencies, the President has experienced considerable difficulty, as his public statements indicate, in finding individuals competent to serve as executives in these and similar agencies.

RECRUITING BUREAU DIRECTORS

Directors of the permanent bureaus of the Federal government make up the largest group of executives to be chosen. Yet little is heard of the difficulties of locating competent individuals and inducing them to accept appointments to these positions. Probably two thirds of these positions are filled by the promotion of individuals from within the permanent civil service ranks. A significant proportion of the remaining appointments are made by the selection of a professional person from without the government, e.g., the appointment of a professor of economic geology to the position of Director of the Bureau of Mines. In some instances appointments result from partisan political pressures or as a result of the vigorous urging of groups vitally interested in the work of a particular bureau or office. In the filling of these positions each department head has the aid of the departmental personnel staff, now headed in several executive departments by a permanent career "Administrative Assistant Secretary."

EXECUTIVES FOR EMERGENCY AGENCIES

In contrast, the heads of the newly established emergency agencies have been drawn predominantly from without the ranks of the government; indeed only Robert C. Goodwin, Director of the Office of Defense Manpower, was serving within the government at the time of his appointment. Three forces have been instrumental in bringing these particular individuals (with the exception of Mr. Goodwin) into these posts. The prestige of the office of the Presidency has induced such men as Charles E. Wilson, Eric Johnston, and Cyrus W. Ching to take the posts they have occupied. Second, the pressure of such economic groups as the Business Advisory Council of the Department of Commerce, the U.S. Chamber of Commerce, the National Association of Manufacturers, trade associations, and others has persuaded men to accept these responsibilities. Similarly, leaders from the oil and power industries singled out Bruce Brown and George W. MacManus and then helped Secretary of the Interior Chapman to persuade them to serve as, respectively, Administrator of the Petroleum Administration for Defense and Administrator of the Defense Electric Power Administration. Third, personal friendship and acquaintance have influenced other executives to serve —and given key mobilization leaders aides in whom they had confidence and with whom they could work effectively. For example, their personal acquaintance with Charles E. Wilson accounted for the service within the Office of Defense Mobilization of General Lucius Clay and Sidney Weinberg; similarly, their personal acquaintance with William H. Harrison accounted for the employment in the Defense Production Administration and National Production Authority of a number of the principle executives.

During the early months of the emergency, the recruitment of executives to head the bureaus and divisions within each emergency agency went on feverishly.[2]

[2] An illustration of the feverish activity is a letter addressed to

Each agency had to do its own recruitment of executives. The recruitment had to take place even before the organization of the agency had been formulated and the posts for which executives were being recruited precisely identified. Those responsible for recruitment have, in many instances, with their right hand made determinations as to functional problems, directed the activities of such staffs as already existed, dealt with the Congress, and interpreted their actions to the press, while with their left hand they sought desperately—usually by long-distance telephone—for people with the competence and stature required to fill top-level positions within the agency. Desperation has resulted more than once in several recruiting officers besieging the same private employer with the request to release one of his assistants on a single day. It has resulted in helter-skelter recruitment by all the executive staff; one agency head pleaded with all of his top-level associates in a staff meeting "to get out and find good men." It has resulted in the waste of competent executives who have reported for work to superiors who had not known that they were coming, who they were, or what they were particularly fitted to do.

The executive recruitment process has varied from one agency to another. In some emergency agencies the original administrators were assisted by a "cadre" of

---

Mr. Sidney J. Weinberg, then principal assistant to Mr. Charles E. Wilson, Director of Defense Mobilization. This letter from the Director of Personnel of the Office of Price Stabilization thanked Mr. Weinberg for his desire to be employed in the OPS but regretted that there was no current need for his services!

permanent civil servants who were "loaned" or "inherited" to aid in establishing the agency and in assembling potential executives; where this was the case, the administrator and the agency have greatly benefited. In other agencies, where specialists in the techniques of executive recruiting were used, a more orderly job was done, and apparently men better fitted for the jobs were obtained. But in still other agencies, where the task of executive recruitment was delegated to a personal confidante of the administrator unskilled in executive recruitment, the results were notably discouraging. In still another agency the administrator himself has endeavored to fill most executive positions by personal consultation with industrial advisory committees and leaders of industry, with obviously little success.

Key positions in several emergency agencies were not filled promptly because the administrator humanly wanted to find individuals of competence whom he personally knew and could work with effectively. Often the administrator finally accepted an individual with whom he was not previously acquainted; frequently this was an individual from within the government ranks with whose work he became familiar by virtue of proximity; at other times this was an individual designated by an industrial group or by a mutual acquaintance in the business world whose recommendation substituted for the administrator's own personal acquaintanceship with the prospective appointee. But the repeatedly manifested desire of the heads of emergency agencies to have about them individuals with whom they, their friends, or their business associates are acquainted offers a distinguishing characteristic of this problem.[3] In developing better methods and institutional machinery to obtain the needed executives, ways must be found to expand the top executive's personal acquaintanceship and to build his confidence in individuals with especial competence who have been recruited by channels beyond his acquaintanceship. In one instance the personnel directors of a group of private corporations came to Washington to consult with the Administrator of an executive agency. They were told of the agency's needs and were asked to suggest names of competent people on the staffs of their companies who could accept such positions. The results were small, either because the needs of the agency were poorly stated or because the companies represented were unwilling or unable to make their men available. In another instance a letter appealing to the chief executives of more than one hundred corporations to make available trained executives from their staffs to man the Economic Stabilization Administration was dispatched by Charles E. Wilson, Director of Defense Mobilization, and Alan Valentine, the first administrator of the Economic Stabilization Administration. The letter produced many replies, by letter and in person. Some suggested names and a useful source of executives to the staff of this agency.

In none of the emergency agencies is there any evidence of the use of the more scientific methods of selection de-

[3] One executive with whom a prospective appointee was discussed illustrated this problem by saying: "There's no doubt the man has good experience. But I never heard of his company and how am I to know he is the sort of man I would want to go fishing with?"

veloped during recent years both in government and business.[4] Rather the machinery for finding and hiring executives in many agencies is amateurish and inefficient. It cannot be expected to produce qualified individuals and to produce them promptly. The methods that are being used are not equal to the task. That the agencies are operating and that their top-level positions are filled must be attributed primarily to the availability of career civil service employees who could be borrowed and transferred from the permanent agencies of the Federal government to aid those key executives brought in from private business. Of a total of 253 positions classified at Grade 15 and above, in eight Federal departments and agencies, 74.7 percent were filled, during the period between July 1, 1950 and April 1, 1951, by individuals recruited from within the government.[5]

[4] See, for example, the description of the following "promising" methods of selection: agency organization, personnel, and policy test; the Allport-Vernon *Study of Values;* the qualifications investigation; the group oral performance test; the administrative judgment test; and a test of public affairs or current events; in an unpublished study by Milton Mandell, U.S. Civil Service Commission.

[5] The departments and agencies from which this information has been obtained are: State, Commerce (including NPA), Interior (including PAD, DPA, and SFA), Army, Air Forces, Federal Civil Defense Administration, Defense Transport Administration, and the Economic Stabilization Administration.

IV. REASONS FOR REFUSAL

THE disorderly and inefficient methods by which executives are recruited for a number of emergency Federal agencies reflect in some part the general unwillingness of many individuals outside government to accept executive positions in these agencies. Recruiting officials testify that for many of the more important jobs approximately four of every five individuals who are sought out refuse.

Why? Why, when the Federal government establishes new functions made necessary by a world-wide crisis, should individuals refuse to serve in important, influential, prestigious positions tendered them?

Few who refuse to serve could give a single precise reason for their refusal. A man's decision to accept or reject a position of this rank is not easily analyzed, even by himself. It results from a conscious or unconscious balancing of factors—compensation, home, family, prospects for the future, status and prestige, personal interests, and satisfaction with associates. The decision reached by any individual is a composite distilled from such considerations. Yet it is still useful to weigh the reasons most frequently cited by those who refuse top-level Federal jobs. The reasons analyzed in subsequent sections are not mutually exclusive. They are classified into three categories for purposes of analysis and presentation: the most frequently avowed reasons for refusal; the less often stated underlying reasons; and the reasons given by those men whose previous experience in the Federal government would make them especially useful at this time. In assessing the problem of obtaining executive manpower the three categories must be considered together.

AVOWED REASONS

Inadequacy of Compensation. The inadequacy of Federal salaries is frequently given as the reason why men in private business refuse top-level Federal jobs; it is seldom stated as a reason for the refusal of Federal jobs by men serving on college or university faculties or on the staffs of labor organizations. The maximum salary for an executive position in the Federal civil service other than that attached to a position as a member of the President's cabinet was, until recently, $10,000. This top limit was raised in 1948 to a maximum of $10,330.[1] Even more recently the classification of Federal positions was modified to add three grades of positions at the top.[2] The incumbents of the limited number of positions included in this group are paid at the following rates: Grade 16,

[1] Public Law 900, Postal Rate Revision and Federal Employees Salary Act of 1948, July 3, 1948.

[2] Public Law 429, 81st Congress, October 1949.

$12,000; Grade 17, $13,000; and Grade 18, $14,800. The presently effective maximum salary, hence, for executive positions in the Federal civil service is $14,800. Few executive positions are included within this top salary class, and a rigidly limited number of positions are classified above Grade 15.[3]

The refusal of many to accept Federal executive positions is not attributable to a simple unwillingness to work for a salary of from $12,000 to $14,800. As William H. Harrison, then Administrator of the Defense Production Administration in personal conversation succinctly stated: Their refusals are based in many instances on cold, hard facts, and the cold hard facts are mortgages on their homes, insurance premiums to meet, tuition payments for children in college, and all the other fixed payments which constitute the standard of living the would-be-appointee has established for himself and his family.[4]

These "cold, hard facts" reflect the generally higher level of compensation for executives in private business.[5] They indicate that even the greater compensation now

[3] Special authority was granted in the Congressional statutes establishing the Atomic Energy Commission and the Economic Cooperation Administration to compensate a limited number of officials at $15,000 per annum and above. Public Law 585, 79th Congress, The Atomic Energy Act of 1946, August 1, 1946, and Public Law 472, 80th Congress, April 3, 1948.

[4] See Senate Report No. 1113, 80th Congress, 2nd Session, pp. 18–21, and Hearings before the Subcommittee of the Committee on Post Office and Civil Service, U.S. Senate, 80th Congress, 2nd Session, on S. 1537, pp. 34, statement by Dr. Jerome C. Hunsaker, Chairman, National Advisory Committee for Aeronautics.

[5] For a similar point of view, see *Fortune*, October 1950, "Washington's Executive Famine," pp. 73–75. See also p. 71 for comparison of salaries of private and public executives.

attached to Federal executive positions will not induce the successful executive in private business to accept Federal employment. Moreover he is dissuaded by the additional costs involved in moving his family and home to Washington and in finding living quarters in an increasingly congested national capital.

Three results arise from the inadequacy of Federal executive salaries. Relatively few executive positions in emergency agencies are filled by executives from private business; the bulk of these positions are filled by career civil servants transferred from other agencies of the Federal government. Second, a large proportion of those business executives who are induced to serve do so "without compensation." These individuals continue to be compensated by their private employers. In some instances where they accept the compensation attached to the position it is because they possess substantial wealth, or because they are retired and can supplement their Federal compensation by a continuing pension, or because their private employer has granted them a leave of absence with a substantial bonus or "termination payment" to supplement the compensation they will receive from the Federal government. Third, among business executives available for service in the Federal government there is a large proportion of older men.

Inability to Leave Private Affairs. Some men contend that they cannot leave their posts in private business even to accept temporary employment in an emergency agency. They refuse on the grounds that there is no person available to replace them temporarily in their private employment. The able, younger executive, who is particularly needed in the emergency agencies, where the physical demands of the job and the need for flexibility are especially great, often fears that even though his employer might grant him a leave of absence to serve in the Federal government, he would not be able to regain his position and the status he holds in private employment after an extended absence.[6] Some private employers who are willing to grant leaves of absence to men for Federal service frankly admit their inability to guarantee that the individual will regain the intangible status he occupies among his associates at the time he leaves. Finally, the experiences of a few executives who served in Federal jobs during World War II and failed to regain positions with their previous employers are much bruited about among those who seek reasons for refusing to interrupt the even tenor of their ways.

Insecurity. Other men refuse Federal executive positions because of the insecurity of public employment.[7]

[6] *Ibid.*, p. 74: "An individual may be loaned for a temporary job, with seniority and re-employment rights technically guaranteed, only to find himself out of favor upon return. In some mysterious way government service has stigmatized him in the eyes of his colleagues and superiors. He will find it wise to soft-pedal useful things learned in Washington, and instead dredge up as many anecdotes of 'incredible mismanagement' as he can."

[7] Dr. Louis N. Ridenour of the University of Illinois told the Atomic Scientists of Chicago on November 24, 1950: "One of the ways of increasing one's personal effectiveness while rendering public service is to be free of the necessity of relying on a permanent government job for financial security. Because of this we find in the government service large numbers of men with independent financial means." Tom Wallace, the distinguished editor emeritus of *The Louisville Times*, prescribed a similar resource for editorial writers to preserve their freedom to write as they choose. Every writer, he argued, should have a "Go

College and university faculty members who enjoy permanent tenure in their professorial posts, and a goodly number of career civil servants in the permanent Federal departments, refuse to trade their permanent jobs for the uncertainty, if not the insecurity, necessarily associated with an "emergency" agency the function of which will presumably expire at some time in the future.[8] In addition, many businessmen will not forsake their job security. In the words of one utility executive who came to Washington to serve in an "emergency agency" for ninety days (and remained longer), "After thirty years with my company I can't pick up and leave a good position and sacrifice my pension rights even as important and interesting as work in the government is; after all it took me a long time to gain the position and compensation my company pays me—and I have a wife to consider." The security of job tenure and of retirement arrangements is, this recruitment experience suggests, of steadily increasing importance in an economy in which most men work as employees and are dependent throughout their lives on their ability to earn a salary and a subsequent pension. Emergency Federal jobs, accompanied by some prospect of political turnover, offer an inadequate measure of security for many potential appointees.

Abuse of Public Officials. A Middle Western business-

---

to Hell Fund," a savings account to carry himself and family if the writer must resign on grounds of principle. One wonders whether indeed there are "large numbers of men with independent financial means" in the Federal service.

[8] It is recognized that the Federal Civil Service Commission has established "reemployment rights" for those employees of Federal agencies who transfer for the emergency to defense jobs.

man who had been asked to make an able, young assistant available for an important Federal position aptly stated a fourth reason for refusals. The businessman came to Washington to make inquiries of his own before he replied. After a day or two in Washington he advised the "talent scout" who had proferred the invitation substantially as follows: "I recognize my obligation to do what is necessary when my government is in trouble. My associates out West agree that we should make this man available—and we can afford to do so—if he can really do a job. But after two days talking with members of Congress and others here in whom I have confidence, I have decided to advise this man not to accept the job. I know it is important work; I don't doubt he could do it, but I don't intend to have his reputation torn to shreds by any politician, news writer or radio commentator who finds it to his personal advantage to take a shot at him."

On the other hand, a significant group of the more moderate and thoughtful members of Congress believe that: (1) the surveillance of the Congress and the press is essential to the revelation of the activities of the few businessmen who accept Federal jobs to serve their own personal interests; (2) the functioning of Congressional committees by and large has contributed more to the efficiency of the executive branch than to the abuse of individuals; (3) those businessmen who are not willing to stand up before a Congressional committee and the public press to defend their policies and actions just "aren't patriotic enough" or are unfitted temperamentally to serve in government jobs; (4) men accepting positions as Federal executives must recognize that the public service in a representative democracy involves a degree of accountability to the legislature and to the public, unparalleled by any experience in private business.[9]

Similar views are held by leading newspaper writers, radio commentators, and news executives. They decry the irresponsible attacks which their fellows have from time to time launched at public officials. They disavow that sector of the press which exploited the fact that a disaffected daughter of a former executive of the Department of Commerce had been employed by the Russian news agency, Tass and the efforts of Fulton Lewis, radio commentator, to demonstrate by discredited evidence that the late Harry Hopkins had shipped secret documents to Russia.[10] Yet they insist that it is the function of these media of communication constantly to probe for and to publish the facts as they see them. The "facts" which a former businessman-public official believes should be published and the interpretation that should be placed upon them often vary sharply from the "facts" and the interpretation placed upon them by an enterprising and inquiring reporter.

In short, this characteristic of employment in Federal executive posts is not likely to change. The American government—federal, state, and local—operates in an atmosphere of open questioning of government and pub-

[9] In principal part of this summary of an influential body of congressional opinion is based on conversations with Congressman Emmanuel Celler of New York, Senator Paul Douglas of Illinois, and Senator Ralph E. Flanders of Vermont.

[10] See *New York Times,* December 4, 1949, 16:1.

lic officials. Our cultural heritage influences the American people repeatedly to ask: Are the functions being undertaken essential? Are the officials qualified to be where they are?

Yet the significance of this reason for the refusal of individuals to serve must not be overstated. Many who are invited to accept posts below the level of Administrator or head of an agency do not fear this threat. They may recognize it as an undesirable characteristic of public employment but not as a threat to their own individual performance in the Federal government.

Similarly there is little evidence that individuals are deterred from accepting opportunities to serve in the Federal government by the "loyalty" or "security" investigations that are now required. The inquiries of one's friends and business associates that these investigations involve have proved irritating—but not deterring.[11] These investigations have, however, delayed recruitment. Such investigations are time-consuming. They add three weeks or more to the time required to complete the employment of an individual willing to accept a proferred position.

Fear of Legal Reprisal. A few individuals refuse Federal posts because they fear possible legal action against either themselves or their private employer as a result of acts they may take as government officials. Their fears

[11] Few men outside the government are familiar with the bungling injustice with which a small number of Federal employees are brusquely suspended and required to defend themselves against vague "charges," and hence few refuse to serve because of the threat of such investigations.

are founded on a number of Federal criminal statutes which are generally described as "the conflict of interest statutes." [12] Before World War II the problems arising out of the recruitment of "dollar-a-year men" were met by having the Attorney General or the chief legal officer of the recruiting department render an opinion as to the proposed employment. During World War II, to facilitate employment of needed executives, Congress enacted specific statutes exempting persons employed under certain conditions from the application of these statutes. Congress has enacted similar exemptions in the statutes creating the current emergency agencies.[13]

In the Defense Production Act of 1950 the Congress went further. This Act authorized the President to issue regulations granting needed exemptions from the application of the "conflict of interest statutes." The President consequently issued Executive Order 10,182 and Executive Order 10,205. These orders stipulate that the head of an agency must certify that each appointment of an individual to serve "without compensation" is necessary, that the position requires outstanding experience and ability, that the appointee has these qualifications, and that a qualified person to serve on a salary basis is unavailable. They stipulate, too, that individuals serving without compensation shall be appointed "so far as pos-

[12] This group of statutes includes U.S. Code, Title 18, 281, 283, 284, 434, 1914, and Title 5 and 9.

[13] The National Security Act of 1947, the National Industrial Reserve Act of 1948, the Foreign Assistance Act of 1948, the Mutual Defense Assistance Act of 1949, the Selective Service Act of 1948, the Defense Production Act of 1950, and the Federal Civil Defense Act of 1950.

sible . . . to advisory or consultative positions only." [14]

Federal officials, responsible for the drafting of these executive orders, contend that individuals who enter the employ of the defense agencies are amply protected. But some attorneys outside the government argue that "it is a little difficult to see that any relief from the operation of the criminal statutes is afforded by this order" [15] (i.e., Executive Order 10,182). Memoranda and counter-memoranda, written by legal officers within the government, have reassured those businessmen who raise these fears of possible legal action in the future. The net result is that there is little evidence that potential executives refuse positions on these grounds. Moreover, there are few instances in the past in which these criminal statutes have been used to prosecute businessmen who had served their country.

Yet the occupants of such positions were suspect in World War I and in World War II, and they likely will be now. For example, a story in the publication of Labor's League (A.F. of L.) for political Education lists a number of businessmen serving in Federal posts under the heading, "Can a Man Serve Two Masters? Look at Company Paid Men in Government." Two Congressional Committees have indicated their intention of investigating the activities of "w.o.c." appointees. Several newspaper columnists have raised questions as to the objectivity of specific officials.

[14] Executive Order 10,182, Part I, Sec. 102 (a).

[15] Quoted from a memorandum prepared by the staff of one of the nation's best-known legal firms which advises many corporations.

Businessmen serving without compensation may be especially vulnerable to criticism at this time because of the relatively large number of such appointees certified to be necessary in a few emergency agencies and because of the assignment of some businessmen to nonadvisory or consultative posts in which their impartiality will likely be questioned. One wonders, when observing the current use of "w.o.c." men, whether an incident which occurred when the Defense Production Agency moved into the "Old Pension Building" is symbolic. The building had been occupied by the General Accounting Office. Its renovation for the new occupants required extensive cleaning and painting. In a large pile of rubbish was found a sign apparently discarded by the incoming tenants. It read: "No man can accept any hospitality from a contractor and not have the edge of his sense of duty blunted."

UNDERLYING REASONS FOR REFUSAL

The man who refuses to accept a Federal position cannot always indicate why. Underlying his refusal there may be: (a) reasons he would not choose to articulate, (b) other reasons not apparent to himself, and (c) still other reasons he may use in explaining his action to his intimates but not give to the recruiting officer.

Visualizing the Job. Some men refuse Federal positions because they are unable to visualize the nature of the job they are asked to undertake. In many instances this is attributable to the disorderly recruitment methods that prevail. Some governmental administrators contend that in rapidly evolving emergency agencies it is not possible "to lay out each job, but if we can only get good men they'll find their place." For this reason and others many jobs to be filled are not defined. Men are asked to come in for vague "important assignments."

In other instances the prospective appointee cannot comprehend the character of the work to be undertaken. It involves a scope far beyond the bounds of the business enterprise in which he had succeeded. It exceeds his imagination. Hence, through fear of the nature of the assignment, or through an uncertainty as to what is involved, he refuses.

In short, the businessman, in many instances, is unwilling to embark upon a job which is not or cannot be given a precise statement, or a job with a scope far beyond his previous experience.

Is There an Emergency? One businessman replied to the offer of a job: "If this were a shooting war I'd come down Monday morning, but frankly I can't leave my business under the present circumstances." A college professor replied to the offer of an equally important position: "I might be able to come for the second semester but I have promised to teach in the Summer School and I would have to be back here by July 1."

Recruiting officers report a striking difference between the attitudes of potential appointees today and the reactions of those who were sought out during the period following December 7, 1941. Many whose services are sought at this time evidence little concern over the current threat of war or inflation. A few businessmen do not agree that controls over materials, wages, and prices should be invoked. Hence they are not willing to interrupt their personal arrangements to accept positions in the administration of such activities.

Absence of "Drawing Cards." Still others refuse to accept top-level Federal positions because they lack esteem and respect for the heads of the agencies under whose leadership they would work. When Manly Fleischmann was asked to succeed General William H. Harrison as Administrator of the National Production Authority, he demurred. He argued that he, a lawyer, would find it more difficult to recruit business leaders to serve in posts where they were urgently needed than a businessman with outstanding reputation.

Mr. Fleischmann's point is illustrated by the prestige of General George C. Marshall and of Charles E. Wilson, former president of the General Electric Company. The recruitment of executives for the Department of Defense and for those mobilization agencies under Mr. Wilson's immediate aegis has been enhanced by their presence. Paul Hoffman's prestige and personal characteristics facilitated recruitment by the Economic Cooperation Administration of business executives to serve either in posts in Washington or as chiefs of ECA missions to foreign countries.

In other instances the lack of prestige and status on the part of the head of the agency makes difficult the recruitment of executives. Michael DiSalle, Director of the Office of Price Stabilization, came to Washington a relative unknown. He was identified as a politician. His success, after a brief apprenticeship, did not promptly overcome the early handicap of a lack of stature in the eyes of many businessmen who were asked to serve on his staff.

Low Esteem of Public Service. In an era when the Administration in power is of a political faith different from that held by a majority of the country's business leaders it is not unnatural that some men should refuse public service because they differ in political philosophy.

Secretary of the Interior Chapman encountered especial difficulties in recruiting top executives for the Defense Electric Power Administration. Men identified with the private power companies would not associate themselves with an Administration that favored the development of public power. In still other instances, some businessmen report that to accept positions in the government is to brand themselves among their fellows as "odd" or "peculiar." General Harrison has said that some men fear they will be "tagged," as others were "tagged" because of their service during World War II, as "New Dealers."

A related attitude prevalent among business people disparages the general efficiency of public employees and of governmental agencies. One business leader commented, in effect: "Businessmen commonly regard the permanent public officials as mediocre people and it is not to their advantage to be identified with them."

This tendency to depreciate the value of public employment is, unfortunately, not peculiar to businessmen. The President's Scientific Research Board pointed to the same problem in these terms: "Since the earliest studies of prestige of different types of employment, Government jobs, aside from certain elective positions, have ranked low." [16] The Commission on Organization of the Executive Branch, after a review of seven previously published studies, concluded: "The general pattern of opinion, however, indicates that over a period of many years Government has had a definite problem of prestige —a problem which undoubtedly limits the 'drawing power' of Government in a competitive labor market, as well as its ability to retain highly qualified personnel, especially in the top administrative, professional and scientific occupations." [17]

The Commission's staff supplemented this summary of previously published studies by three inquiries addressed to college seniors. A total of 10,200 questionnaires were distributed to students graduating in 1948 from ninety-four colleges and universities.

On the basis of the answers received from 3,448 students it was concluded that:

1. College seniors today are not actively interested in a career in the Federal Service. . . .
2. An important cause of the uncertainty about and rejection of a career in Government is believed to lie in

[16] President's Scientific Research Board, *Science and Public Policy*, A Report to the President (Oct. 4, 1947) by J. R. Steelman, Chairman, III, 142.

[17] Commission on Organization of the Executive Branch, Appendices to Report of the Personnel Policy Committee, p. C-2. See also S. Mailick, "Public Service Prestige: Problem and Paradox," *Public Personnel Review*, July, 1949, p. 155, for a summary review of other studies of the prestige of public employment and the "determinants" of prestige.

the absence of knowledge about Federal employment opportunities and practices. . . .

3. While college seniors feel that they would find greater security in a Government career, this positive benefit is largely overshadowed by their feeling that Government cannot offer adequate financial rewards and promotional opportunity.[18]

These conclusions reflect the static evaluation of the attitudes of young people toward the public service. In the opinion of officials of the United States Civil Service Commission these conclusions are wholly unfounded. These officials submit statistics to show that a fair proportion of the ablest college graduates apply for Federal jobs each year. They indicate that of an annual "crop" of 475,000 recipients of bachelors', professional, and masters' degrees, from two to four percent enter Federal jobs. This total, while approximately equivalent to the proportion that Federal employment makes up of the total labor force, is not impressive. Undoubtedly a significantly larger proportion of college-trained men and women enter the Federal service than a generation ago. Yet when one attempts to assess the over-all distribution of our ablest young men and women, one must doubt that the Federal government yet claims the share which the importance of its role in our civilization makes desirable.

Here, then, are four reasons not often stated but frequently influential in determining whether an individual will accept an assignment with the Federal government: (1) a lack of definition of the job and opportunity of-

[18] Mailick, *loc. cit.*

fered; (2) little concern over the emergency that makes the filling of the position necessary; (3) lack of respect for the heads of the agencies under whom the individuals would serve; and (4) the lack of prestige attached to public employment. The recruiting officer can encounter the usually *stated* reasons for refusal by a prospective appointee. But the reasons summarized here are less easily combated and, as a consequence, perhaps the more influential.

REASONS GIVEN BY THE EXPERIENCED

There are many men and women scattered throughout business enterprise, labor organizations, and academic institutions who served in governmental agencies during World War II. Those who served in the War Production Board, Office of Price Administration, Office of Defense Transportation, Office of Civilian Defense, and War Labor Board during World War II have experience particularly fitting them to help during the current emergency. Yet these men and women frequently refuse to return to important executive positions. Why?

Frustrations of Public Service. Frequently their stated reason is an ill-defined one—"the frustrations of public service."[19] Many private business executives are accustomed to substantial freedom, independence of action, a small enterprise, and relatively simple questions to cope with. They become frustrated by relatively in-

[19] See Robert A. Lovett, "A Business Executive Looks at Government," in *The Public Service and University Education* (Princeton University Press, 1949), p. 73.

flexible civil service provisions designed to prevent illegal appointments.[20] They rail against the "red tape" which both protects the civil servant against public pressures and insures compliance with legislative decisions. They are irritated by the detailed procedures and "clearance" made necessary by the large size of the typical governmental agency. They are unaccustomed to working with scores of specialists; the businessman, particularly he who has been associated with a smaller business, is a generalist. Many who have served found these irritations so frustrating that they refuse to serve in the Federal government again.

"Politics" Involved. Some men who have held Federal jobs attribute their unwillingness to return to "politics." They object to having been called upon to grant undue favors or to bend their policy decisions for partisan purposes. At times, however, their statements suggest that they object to the necessity while in public office of conforming with political decisions, that is, decisions by the established legislative body or the elected executive. The term "politics," however, by which they articulate their reason for refusal, is seldom given precise statement.

For a time this objection was focused on the Office of Price Stabilization. The Director of this Office, a career politician, had served previously as Mayor of Toledo, Ohio, and had run for elective office in his home state on several occasions. Early in his administration one of

[20] Lovett, *loc. cit.*: "I think there is fairly general agreement among the wartime administrators obtained from private business that our civil service system constituted a major problem in their efforts to set up an effective organization in a period of crisis."

his principal aides, a retired military officer, resigned on the ground that he was unwilling to participate in an administration which would "take politics into every home." The Democratic senators from Mississippi added fuel to the fire. They charged that jobs with this agency had been "sold" to individuals in their state. These charges were denied, yet they caused businessmen and academic people to conclude that they would prefer to have no part in this and other emergency agencies.

There is little evidence, however, that party politics plays any significant part in the selection of individuals for top-level positions. Interviews with most of the "talent scouts" for Federal emergency agencies reveal little or no concern with the prospective appointee's party affiliations. Doubtless for positions of lesser rank in the field offices, outside Washington, party affiliation has greater influence in determining appointments.

Discouraging Working Conditions. Individuals who served during World War II remember Washington, congested and hot, and the conditions under which many had to work. Offices were crowded; many executives were grouped with their staffs in noisy, open, ill-fitted quarters—a converted apartment house, a loft building, hotel rooms, or the "temporary" buildings constructed during World War I. The rapid growth of governmental agencies meant that some officials had to be moved frequently. Remembering these handicaps they demur when asked to accept a position for this emergency.

In considerable part, the same crowded conditions are already duplicated. Offices of the National Production Authority and the Defense Production Administration were, within the first few months of their existence, moved four times. At a critical time in the development of these agencies both were located in the antique "Pension Building." While they worked, partitions were being built and the walls painted. Meanwhile they contemplated the necessity of recruiting up to 4,000 additional employees with no adequate space in which to house them. The Economic Stabilization Agency, housed in a World War I "temporary building," has been even more crowded, in no more desirable space and confronted with the same distressing necessity of recruiting thousands of additional workers without space in which to house them.

Memory of Criticism. Other men remember the criticism they received while serving during World War II. Men and women who served in the Office of Price Administration during the early 1940's most often voice this objection to serving again. Theirs was an unpopular mission. They were criticized by the press, the Congress, and the businesses and individuals with which they dealt. Having experienced this criticism they conclude in the words of Paul Porter, former Administrator of OPA, that "no man should be expected to place his life in jeopardy for his government a second time."

These four reasons duplicate in some part reasons given for refusal by others who have never served. None of these four reasons is customarily the primary reason although each influences some men to refuse. Their significance lies only in that they constitute some of the obstacles which prevent the recruitment of individuals possessing skills and experience of especial value.

V. THE NEED FOR ACTION NOW

DESPITE the difficulties that have been encountered in recruiting men and women to serve in the top-level positions, essential military supplies are being procured, our transportation, petroleum, and power facilities are being mobilized, minerals and materials are being controlled, and substantial steps have been taken toward the stabilization of prices and wages.

But many of these positions have been filled only after undue effort and lost time. Some posts are still unfilled. In the early summer of 1951 the original sweeping price and wage stabilization orders still had not been supplemented by more considered, precise orders that would enable businessmen to know better where they stood. If anyone wondered when such supplementary orders would be forthcoming, he might have been told, "As soon as we can obtain a man from your industry to come in and help draft the order." Some procurement plans, mobilization plans, and control orders would have been issued earlier to relieve the vacuum of information that existed in many fields—if a larger number of competent, top-level personnel had been available. And this shortage of the essential management and policy-forming talent was not relieved promptly. In the military departments hundreds of additional men, skilled in contract negotiation and production, were needed. The control of prices required many more men and women to write and administer regulations than could be recruited in time. The establishment of a controlled-materials plan required dozens of competent industrial specialists in 1951, and its establishment promptly on schedule was a tribute to the capabilities of an ingenious few. Within the last half of 1951 the need for experienced and knowledgeable executives expanded far beyond the needs apparent in the period following the outbreak in Korea.

Even before the expansion of these agencies was well under way, a significant proportion of the executives then serving had left! In the Office of Program and Requirements of the Defense Production Administration, the director and deputy director who originally organized this unit left within six months. They were replaced by five executives, four of them borrowed from private business enterprises, the fifth from an academic institution. No one of this "second crop" of executives remained through the second six months—only the college professor accepted compensation from the government for his services.

The executive staffs of the Office of Price Stabilization, the Defense Transport Administration, and other emergency agencies have been made up of many men who considered their assignments as temporary and of secondary importance to their private employments. In some agencies a relatively large proportion of all top-level positions have been filled by "consultants," i.e., individuals hired from without the government to serve on a *per diem* basis. These individuals, in a minority of instances, served in an established executive position on an indefinite basis. In other instances, they served part time, i.e., three or four days a week, or two, three, or four hours each day.

In addition, many key posts are still filled by men recruited from, and more often "loaned" by, businesses or industries with which, as public officials, they are obligated to deal. For example, the Office of Price Stabilization official in charge of price regulations for the apparel industry (in 1951) was borrowed from a leading firm in this industry. His aide, who specializes in women's woven underwear, is "on loan" from Barbizon, one of the principal competing manufacturers in this field. A succession of five or more chiefs of the Iron and Steel Division in the National Production Authority have been loaned by their companies, the major companies in the steel industry. The acting director of the Equipment and Materials Division of the Defense Transport Administration for most of 1951 was on loan from the American Car and Foundry Company. He actively promoted, for the Defense Transport Administrator, a plea that the NPA make available sufficient steel to build 10,000 freight cars a quarter; his firm meanwhile is engaged in the production of freight cars. There is no evidence that this individual, or any of those referred to, has taken advantage of his position. Rather there are numerous illustrations of individuals in such positions endeavoring scrupulously to perform their functions in a wholly objective manner. Yet the heads of agencies in which businessmen are used in positions where they can provide information or make decisions of benefit to the firm from which they are temporarily detached will persistently be vulnerable to public criticism.

Our society is confronted with the dreary prospect of living, for as long as we can see in the future, under the threat of overwhelming war or, at best, in a drawn-out state of emergency never dramatized by a general "shooting war." A temporary, part-time staff occupying top-level positions in which some men will be able to make, if they choose, decisions of great advantage to their permanent employers, is obviously not ideally fitted to organize and direct the mobilization of this nation's resources. Yet it will be increasingly difficult to induce competent executives to come into the government. Executives now serving for limited periods will have to be replaced. Some executives will die, some will fail, and others will resign. A constant flow of new executives will be required; whence is it to come?

VI. AN EMERGENCY PROGRAM

WHAT can be done to obtain the executive talent that is needed for the immediate emergency? And what can be done to overcome the reasons which cause men to refuse Federal jobs in which they could contribute to the public welfare?

CREATING AWARENESS

To procure the needed executives, a realization of the critical nature of the current emergency must be created. This country's business leaders must understand and accept ungrudgingly the necessity of making available for civilian public service some of their ablest executives. Relatively few businessmen now yield their aides because they are already concerned about the current emergency. A few leaders among business and professional men must accept the responsibility of convincing their fellows that governmental efforts to build our national defenses and to control inflation are of such consequence to the business community that they should loan some of their most talented aides.

Other businessmen will be induced to aid by the tradition that civilian public service is an obligation when the issues of the day necessitate their participation. The Adamses of New England, the Hughes, the Roots, and the Stimsons of New York, the LaFollettes and their associates in Wisconsin, the Bryans, the Byrds, and the Randolphs of Virginia, and still other families have long been identified with volunteer civilian public service of the highest order of patriotism.[1] This tradition will influence some businessmen, lawyers, and others to serve, where and when they are needed in the civilian public service, with a fervor and selflessness equal to that desire which motivates other men to serve in the armed forces in time of war. They must, however, be convinced that public service in these defense agencies is nonpartisan in character.

Other business leaders can be persuaded to aid by the pragmatic argument that the individual who serves in a top-level position will be of greater value to his corporate employer when he returns. The value of a knowledge of governmental institutions, "how to get around in Washington," and of the personalities in key government positions will suffice to obtain the aid of many corporation executives. Their appreciation of such ex-

[1] In his autobiography, *The Education of Henry Adams*, Adams writes of the tradition in New England society down to 1850 that required the ablest professional men to accept public office. "It was the old Ciceronian idea of government by *the best* that produced the long line of New England statesmen."

perience must not be confused with the self-seeking desire of a few corporate executives to place their aides where they can influence decisions to the employer's advantage or where they are privy to information not available to competing businesses.

A climate of opinion must be developed in business that recognizes both the nature of the continuing emergency and the need for executives to manage important public functions. The creation of this climate will require the cooperation of the daily press, the magazines, the trade journals, the radio and television. Such agencies as the American Newspaper Publishers' Association, the National Association of Broadcasters, the American Society of Newspaper Editors, and the Advertising Council should be enlisted promptly. In addition, to make this appeal effective, the full cooperation of the major business and labor organizations is essential. Indeed, this opinion-forming task should be carried out by and through such agencies as the American Federation of Labor, the American Management Association, the Congress of Industrial Organizations, the National Industrial Conference Board, the National Association of Manufacturers, and the U.S. Chamber of Commerce. With a minimum expenditure and a persuasive statement of the problem, an effective appeal for the service of our ablest men and women in the Federal government could be disseminated effectively through these influential institutions.

ESSENTIAL GOVERNMENTAL ACTION

Such an appeal is desirable—even essential. But four positive steps must be taken expeditiously by the Federal government.

1. Utilizing Career Executives. Approximately three-fourths of all executive jobs in defense activities are filled by individuals previously employed in other Federal agencies. Yet the presence of career civil servants in these emergency agencies cannot be attributed to any orderly process of seeking out the government's ablest career men and women and bringing them to the attention of the heads of emergency agencies. Rather those who are found in these emergency agencies either were employed in an older government agency which was transferred en masse to a newly constituted emergency agency (e.g., the Office of Industry and Commerce of the Department of Commerce became the Bureau of Industry Operations of the National Production Authority) or they are, in substantial part, the "drifters" and "opportunists" who grasp the opportunities offered by the needs of these new agencies. A minority of those now employed in the emergency agencies were sought out as the best qualified individuals that could be found for the positions.

The Federal government's most critical manpower need at the moment is for executives in these emergency agencies. Hence, a planned method of bringing together individuals with particular experience and competence in governmental activities and in the jobs requiring such talents in the emergency agencies is needed. The government must create machinery which will make more effective utilization of the competent manpower it now has. This will prove difficult for two reasons. First, businessmen serving in top-level jobs tend to disparage the competence of men whose repudiations have been established within the Federal civil service—unless the governmental career man is recommended by a fellow businessman. Second, the ablest career executives in the Federal service are firmly entrenched in jobs where they are needed and usually well satisfied. The Federal Civil Service Commission has taken two steps to facilitate the utilization of career employees. The reestablishment of "reemployment rights" for those permanent employees who leave nondefense agencies to serve in defense agencies will encourage and facilitate the movement of those individuals who will take or have cause to take the initiative to find another job.[2] The second step is the announcement of an "Executive Placement Program," which invites career administrators to take a competitive examination, open only to Federal administrators, to demonstrate their capacity for higher-grade administrative work.

Both efforts fall short of the real need for identifying the most capable career administrators. These efforts tend rather to encourage those who temperamentally or, because of dissatisfaction with their present job, are prone "to make a change." The need is not to create

[2] U.S. Civil Service Commission, Departmental Circular No. 653, "Standards and procedures for grant of reemployment rights—Revision of Program," February 23, 1951.

temporarily greater opportunities for some career employees. It is to find the most competent individuals available for executive positions in the emergency agencies and to convince businessmen-administrators of their especial skills. The Federal government cannot logically demand that business, professional, and academic people interrupt their personal careers to serve if it will not make an equivalent effort to utilize, to the maximum advantage, the executive manpower it already possesses.

2. *Frank Countenance of Service without Compensation.* Secondly, the government must accept frankly and fully the necessity of utilizing as executives in key Federal jobs men and women drawn from industry temporarily who will continue to be compensated by their private employers.[3] This recommendation is made despite the evidence that there will be increasing criticism of the use of such individuals. This recommendation is made, too, despite the conviction that the value of the services of such men is reduced by limited responsibility to their public employer and, especially, by the necessity of placing careful checks upon the assignments and decision-making responsibilities of such officials. It is made because of the impossibility of overcoming those

[3] After both World War I and World War II there was an obvious reaction against the employment of individuals serving without compensation. Yet in both emergencies such individuals were required, and the need for "special industry know-how" makes their use at this time inevitable. For summary of the experience during World War II, see "Dollar-A-Year and Without Compensation Personnel Policies of the War Production Board and Predecessor Agencies, August 1939 to November 1949," *Historical Reports on War Administration: War Production Board*, Special Study No. 27.

financial reasons–inadequacy of compensation, inability to forsake private affairs, and the insecurity of public employment—which cause many men to refuse public jobs. It is made, more importantly, because of the urgent need, in a government increasingly concerned with the regulation and control of private business enterprise, for individuals who are competent executives and simultaneously thoroughly familiar with the functioning of American business.

To obtain a continuing supply of individuals with such business "know-how" to serve without compensation justifies a thorough study of existing legislation governing such employment. Such a study might help Congress to wipe out the accretion of confusing "conflict of interest statutes." It should yield a more intelligible statute imposing those few restraints and requiring those few disclosures essential to the public interest and to the individual. In addition, such a statute should establish forthrightly the need for the services of such individuals and the conditions under which they shall be utilized. It should serve to force all Federal agencies to exercise greater care in the assignment of w.o.c. personnel to positions which do not involve dealings or decisions affecting their personal interests. Such a statute might well, in addition, encourage individuals to serve in this manner by authorizing the deduction, as a professional or business expense, from taxes on the individual's gross annual income up to $5,000 or one fourth of his gross annual income, whichever is greater, where it is demonstrated that by virtue of the individual's service in the Federal government he incurs added and unusual expense incident to maintaining living quarters in Washington and elsewhere.

3. Improved Recruitment Methods. The third step to be taken by the Federal government is a thorough appraisal of existing methods of executive recruitment. The disorderly and even chaotic methods and practices prevailing at present in some emergency agencies must be supplanted by well-considered and planned methods of identifying qualified executives now serving outside the government, of making the most effective bid for their services to the individuals and to their employers, and of inducting them into the positions in which they are to serve. These executives, of course, will also require assurance that they shall be used at their maximum capacity.

The techniques of executive recruitment are reasonably well established. There have been notable illustrations both within the Federal government (in the Economic Cooperation Administration and the Atomic Energy Commission) and outside the government (by a number of management consulting firms as well as by business corporations) of successful executive recruitment by planned and considered methods.[4] These methods involve at least these essential components:

a) A clear definition of responsibilities of and personal qualifications required for each position to be filled.

[4] A helpful adaptation of these methods to the task of selecting presidential appointees is contained in a letter addressed to John F. Mee, formerly a special assistant on the White House staff, by Lawrence A. Appley, American Management Association, July 26, 1950.

b) A comprehensive review of the fields in which potentially qualified individuals may be found to develop a list of prospective appointees from which the executive may select.

c) The continuing performance of both the foregoing tasks (analysis of position and identification of potential appointees) by an individual possessing a high order of talent, wide acquaintanceship among business people, and, if possible, previous specialized experience in the recruitment of executives.

d) The regular interchange of experience among the officials responsible for executive recruitment in each of the several emergency agencies. Such interchange should result in the improvement of techniques; establish cooperation among these officials in identifying qualified individuals and in persuading these individuals and their employers to make their services available; and minimize competing and duplicating appeals by several recruiting officers to the same business firm.

e) The deliberate acceptance of the task of executive recruitment by the chief executive of each emergency agency as an immediate and continuing function of major importance.

f) The establishment by each chief executive, with the aid of his assistant on executive recruitment, of committees or panels of consultants who are the leaders in the specialized fields from which individuals are needed, for the purpose of recommending individuals with especial skill and possessing those character and personality traits which will likely enable them to serve effectively as public officials.

g) The institution of well-considered, informal methods of acquainting executives who are brought into the Federal government with the objectives of the agency and of making them understand the organizations in which they will be working. This effort to acquaint the incoming executive should be made very promptly after his entry upon duty and should make clear the positive values and the ways of working with such agencies as the Congress, the White House, the Civil Service Commission, the Bureau of the Budget, and the General Services Administration.

No agency of the Federal government now provides the institutional leadership which might insure the effective recruitment of needed executives. Informal relationships obtain between individuals responsible for recruitment in each of the emergency agencies. Occasionally these individuals contact the Civil Service Commission. Less often these individuals contact the Administrative Assistant to the President responsible for personnel activities. There is an urgent need for strong leadership which would aid these agencies to improve their methods—and their results—in recruiting executives. There is need, too, for some focal point where those businessmen and others who desire to volunteer their services may obtain information. Now they must apply to each emergency agency with consequent loss of time, duplication of effort, and frustrating results. The organizational logic of the Federal government suggests that this leadership should be manifested by the Civil Service Commission. There is, however, a strong objection among businessmen to dealing with the "civil service." Hence it may be necessary to establish some independent agency at the level of the Executive Office in order to coordinate and improve prevailing executive recruitment practices; provide a central office where men from outside the government may volunteer; and sell aggressively to the emergency agencies the services of the most competent men from among those who volunteer.

4. Rotation of Service. The recruitment of executives must be planned with a view to providing a constant staff of executives for an indefinite period. The present crisis may, unfortunately, last for a decade or a generation. Governmental agencies cannot be manned indefinitely by "borrowing" men from private firms for a few months at a time. Hence, it is high time that the recruitment of executives from without the government be planned in such a manner as to fix a minimum period of service for each executive and to provide for his replacement by a qualified individual before that period of service has expired. Even as young men are drafted into the armed services for approximately two years, so business executives and professional people may be persuaded to accept important responsibilities in the civilian public service for definite periods of a year or more. The soldier's place is taken by another man recruited and trained on schedule to replace the young man whose period of service elapses. So the business executive might expect to be relieved at a stipulated time and that a replacement will have been trained by the time he leaves.

Such a program of rotation would facilitate the performance of the public business. It also would enable the private business to order its arrangements. The private employer could better allow for the absence of one or more executives if more definitely scheduled assignments were made. The individual who comes to Washington as an executive would be introduced to the job by his predecessor and have some opportunity to learn before he is asked to undertake an important responsibility. In turn, he would obligate himself to train his successor.

The development of such a program of rotation demands the thinking through of a myriad of details, complexities, and obstacles. But the indefinite mobilization of this nation makes such a program an essential part of an efficient and economical use of our most valuable and most talented manpower. Moreover, such a system would materially reduce the demands made upon each individual and those employers who contribute the services of their staff members.

In summary, the answer to question number 4, posed on page 8 is that it will be necessary to meet this emergency, as the United States has met other emergencies, on a "minuteman" basis. To obtain the executive talent that is needed immediately, it is essential:

1) To create an awareness, especially among business executives, of the urgent need for capable men in top-level Federal jobs;
2) To utilize, to an even greater degree than as yet,

the most capable men and women among the career civil servants;

3) Frankly to encourage the service of many individuals from outside the government without compensation, and to review and revise existing laws and regulations to assure the protection of such individuals;
4) To improve promptly the methods used in recruiting executives from outside the government;
5) To develop a plan for the rotation of individuals from outside the government in top-level jobs.

VII. MEETING THE CONTINUING NEED

NO matter how effective techniques are developed for the procurement of key executives as each successive emergency develops, there is a continuing and expanding need for an efficient and mobile corps of permanent administrators within the Federal government. Seventeen years ago Leonard White wrote:

> The government ought not to be forced to rely on either dollar-a-year men or on temporary loans from American colleges and universities. In a period when it is one of the main responsibilities of government to make the rules of the business game and to supervise their enforcement, public confidence demands the careful balance that a disinterested administrative class, properly trained, could give. Neither is it clear that men from the colleges and universities, called upon at short notice and suddenly transplanted for brief periods, can be expected to give the long-time results that a permanent corps of trained administrators should produce.[1]

The current emergency eloquently reinforces Dr. White's conclusion. And it emphasizes the importance

[1] "Toward a New U.S. Civil Service," *Fortune* (November 1934), p. 76.

of finding ways of developing within the Federal service a more adequate and more respected corps of executives to man the Federal establishments and to provide administrative leadership in times of emergency, even while ways and means are developed to bring more businessmen, experienced in the conduct of the enterprises to be regulated and controlled, into the positions where they, too, are needed.

ESSENTIAL PUBLIC AWARENESS

The creation of an awareness of this urgent personnel need of the Federal government is the first step essential to this end. This requires a persistent and planned effort to develop a greater appreciation of the role of government, the importance of public employment, and the desirability of career opportunities in the Federal government. The responsibility for the development of this awareness must be shouldered by government itself. But the responsibility should be shouldered, too, by this country's schools, colleges, and universities. They have a responsibility for interpreting to the American people the changing role of government, the need for able public servants, and the satisfying opportunities that may be found in public employment.

PRIMARY NEED FOR ABLEST YOUTH

The primary personnel need of government will continue to be the procurement each year of an increasing share of the ablest young men and women for junior professional, scientific, technical, and administrative posts.

Government attracts from 2 to 4 percent of the graduates of the colleges, universities, and technical schools each year. The number is insufficient. The proportion of the total graduating each year that enters the Federal service must be substantially increased as the role of government grows.

The Federal government has made an increasing effort over the past fifteen years to attract a larger number of able young people. The Civil Service Commission has improved its selection techniques and has made a more positive effort to recruit able college graduates. These efforts have brought results; in 1951 approximately 12,000 were recruited. There is good reason to doubt the accuracy of the conclusion—arrived at by the Task Force on Federal Personnel of the Commission on Organization of the Executive Branch—that "there is little systematic intake of capable young people at the bottom of the 'career ladder' throughout the Federal service." [2] But the Task Force's recommendation, that an unpaid commission, appointed by the President, should work out a plan to place greater emphasis on the attraction of first-rate young men and women to junior professional, scientific, technical, and administrative posts, still deserves attention. The acceptance of this recommendation would constitute an important step not only toward achieving a solution but

[2] *Task Force Report on Federal Personnel* (Appendix A), January 1949, p. 34: "Since 1934 the Civil Service Commission has attempted to stimulate the agencies into appointing a number of outstanding young people each year by establishing registers of individuals capable of development for future key professional and administrative positions. The program made excellent progress before the war but has had a discouraging acceptance during the past three years (i.e., 1945–48)."

toward the development of the public awareness urgently needed.

The outline of such a plan is obvious. There is an annual turnover in the Federal service of approximately 500,000 individuals. The filling of these posts should result in bringing into the Federal service up to 25,000 able and carefully selected young people each year. The Civil Service Commission, to accomplish such a goal, must seek out, more aggressively than heretofore, up to 10 percent of this country's annual crop of college graduates. Then it must "market" these individuals to each of the departments and agencies. To insure this annual infusion of young men and women, the Commission should be authorized to identify a number of positions to be filled only through appointment from "career entry registers." Opportunities for manual, clerical, and stenographic workers in the service could be provided by enabling them to take examinations to gain equivalent status. But the basic idea is that the Federal government's need for an increasing share of the ablest people entering the labor market each year is more important to the public good than to theoretical advantages of a competitive system which does not bring in an adequate supply of the nation's ablest youth.

RETAINING AND DEVELOPING THE ABLEST

Equally important is the development of vastly improved methods for the retention, development, and promotion of Federal employees. Indeed, a positive effort to recruit an increasing number of the ablest young people our society produces implies the development of methods for their promotion as they demonstrate their promised capacity. A program to achieve this end was recommended by the Hoover Commission Task Force on Personnel.[3] It provided for (a) increased compensation, (b) the provision of nonmonetary incentives for at least scientific and professional personnel, (c) the development of career promotion programs, and (d) the development of career training programs.

Since these recommendations were made, the enactment of "The Position Classification and Pay Act of 1949" and the "Classified Employee's Pay Act of 1951" have raised the level of compensation for Federal positions, but neither Act provides, as the Task Force recommended, for "a permanent plan . . . for keeping all salary levels, fixed by law, properly adjusted." Moreover, the legislation raising Federal salary levels limits the number of positions whose incumbents can be compensated at $12,000 and above. Meanwhile a persistent rise in the cost of living has pushed the salaries for comparable positions in private business still further above Federal levels.

The differential between executive salaries in private and public employment is revealed by a study of the compensation of executives in 865 private corporations in 1949.[4] In 1949 the effective ceiling of Federal salaries other than for members of the Cabinet and a few Commissions was $10,330. It is assumed that the highest-paid

[3] *Ibid.* (Appendix A), pp. 29–42.
[4] "Compensation and Pensions for Executives," *Studies in Personnel Policy*, No. 111, National Industrial Conference Board.

executive and the second-highest-paid executive in the typical private corporation are to be compared with the Secretaries and Assistant Secretaries of Federal departments; hence, the following table analyzes the annual salaries (exclusive of bonuses, shares of profits, or pension contributions) paid to the third-highest-paid executive in each of 865 corporations in 114 industries.

5 percent were paid less than $11,000 per annum
2 percent were paid from $11,000 to $13,999 per annum
31 percent were paid from $14,000 to $27,999 per annum
60 percent were paid $28,000 per annum or more

In summary terms, in 1949, 93 percent of this group of executives in private employment were paid salaries (exclusive of bonuses, profits, pensions, etc.) in excess of the maximum Federal salary at that time.

Raising Ceiling for Salaries. There remains, hence, the urgent need for raising the salaries of top-level positions in the Federal service. This is essential to retain indefinitely the most capable of those now employed. It is essential also to provide a more attractive future for those seeking a career now and in the future within the Federal service. At present a young man who enters the Federal government at an annual salary of $3,410 can look forward to a maximum salary, after a lifetime of service, of $14,800; the range between entry and final salaries is drastically limited—much more limited than in many fields of private business. The ceiling for Federal salaries should be raised to at least $25,000 per annum and the number of positions to be classified in the grades to which the higher salaries are attached should be limited only by the characteristics of the positions—not by the arbitrary fixing of a specific number of positions, either by the Congress or the President.

Establishment of Nonmonetary Incentives. Such revision of Federal salaries should be accompanied by the establishment of additional nonmonetary incentives. For scientific, professional, and administrative personnel these incentives should include the extension of "present privileges of (1) writing on government time and publishing with authorship credit; and (2) attending and participating in professional meetings [5] at the government expense." [6] In addition, these incentives should include sabbatical leaves; the interchange of personnel between government, business, and academic institutions; such extra salary incentives as provision for the education of children; and entertainment allowances.

Sabbatical leaves are relatively common for academic personnel. They are used, as well, by the British civil service to broaden the experience of key people. They are needed here especially for this latter purpose—the broadening of the experience of key career people in scientific, professional, and administrative positions. The current emergency eloquently demonstrates that the typical Federal executive lacks breadth of experience and recognition, particularly in areas outside the government itself. It is this particular inadequacy that sabbatical leaves

[5] *Task Force Report on Federal Personnel* (Appendix A), p. 42.

[6] S. 2111, a bill now before the Senate of the U.S., would authorize the privilege proposed here, Sec. 11(e).

should be designed to overcome. For example, individuals above the rank of GS-13 might be entitled to a year's leave of absence after five years' service. They should be given wide latitude to determine how they shall spend their year's leave but expected to broaden their experience and their associations rather than to increase their specialized knowledge of the field in which their governmental work falls.[7]

A particularly effective means of broadening the experience of the individual would be to relate such leaves to a continuing interchange of governmental, academic, and business personnel. Such interchange will more readily be worked out in the scientific and professional fields, but it is equally important that there be developed an interchange of personnel in the administrative and management fields. Scientific people would benefit by a year spent in academic study or in the research laboratories of industrial enterprises. Similarly, administrators would benefit by advanced study in the fields of economics, political science, or administration, and especially by the opportunity of participating in the administration of private business enterprises. Such experience would broaden the professional contacts of governmental officials, acquaint them with contrasting environments, and build up a greater mutual understanding between government and the business and academic communities.

Still other incentives are needed. Many men who leave,

[7] S. 2111, a bill now before the Senate of the U.S., would authorize executive agencies to grant such leave "at full or part pay," Sec. 11 (d).

after starting on a career in the public service, do so better to provide for the education of their children. Since it seems unlikely that Federal salaries will be materially increased, there is need for the consideration of other means of providing for the education of these children. The creation of a large number of generous scholarships to be awarded on a competitive basis to the children of public employees of any level would provide a substantial added incentive.[8]

A further incentive, of lesser significance, would be the provision of entertainment allowances. Most Federal officials in the higher ranks find it necessary, from time to time, to entertain businessmen and others with whom their work brings them in contact. They are entertained frequently by such individuals at the expense of the companies represented. Yet they can reciprocate only at their personal expense and from a rigidly limited personal income. If the heads of departments and agencies were authorized to reimburse members of their executive staffs for legitimate expenditures for entertainment, this would place on the government an expense fairly charged against public funds, would increase the real compensation of a number of Federal officials, and would enhance the stature of the positions they occupy.

The greatest incentive to attract and to retain young men and women would be higher salaries, particularly for those positions at the top of the Federal service to which they aspire. But salaries alone will not solve this

[8] This proposal should be viewed in relation to other current proposals for Federally supported scholarships for college education open to all high school graduates.

problem. Moreover, the top salaries of public officials will never equal the maximum salaries paid in private business. The opinion of the great majority of citizens, whose earnings are low, and the inherited concepts of government and the worth of public officials will fix a lower ceiling on earnings in the public service. The man or woman who enters upon a career in the Federal government recognizes this fact. He is attracted, in many instances, by the interesting and significant nature of the work. But experience indicates that the ablest among them will not indefinitely forsake the prospect for larger earnings unless there are compensating advantages. More attractive salaries, regular sabbatical leaves, the prospect of the broadening associations made possible by periodic interchange with business or academic institutions, the assurance of an education for their children, and the provision for essential entertainment expense would, taken together, materially increase the holding power of these positions. If in addition the general public could be made aware of the increasing importance and complexity of positions in the public service, an increasing number of competent individuals could be attracted and retained in the Federal service.

IDENTIFICATION OF POTENTIAL EXECUTIVES

Even if the ceiling in terms of dollars, perquisites, and stature on Federal positions is materially raised, the individual of especial competence must also have some assurance that he will be identified from among the thousands who enter the Federal service and aided to develop his full potentialties. The Task Force on Personnel of the Hoover Commission recommended that "career promotion programs in the Federal Service should be planned and administered by the individual agencies under the leadership of the Civil Service Commission." The following suggestions were made:

a) Each agency should annually audit its key jobs (administrative, scientific, professional, and technical), forecast the probable turnover, and prepare to fill each at the time, present or future, it may become vacant. On the basis of the audit each agency should:
   (1) Identify prospective candidates within the organization to fill key jobs and plan the preparation of such candidates for broader responsibilities.
   (2) Secure the assistance of the Civil Service Commission in selecting candidates, from elsewhere in the service, for those positions which cannot be filled adequately from within the agency.
   (3) Determine the number and type of career trainees who should be appointed currently in order to provide a reservoir of candidates to meet the long-range needs of the agency. This determination should become the basis for annual nationwide examinations of the Civil Service Commission for "career interns."
b) In addition each agency should establish an effective promotion-from-within system which will as-

sure that all qualified employees are considered as openings occur, particularly in the middle and higher grade levels.

The Civil Service Commission is currently endeavoring to interest each Federal department in such programs. But there is no significant evidence of the general acceptance of the principles involved, let alone the establishment of effective programs to identify the more capable entrants into the service and their planned development. There are frequent examples of the rapid rise within the Federal service of younger men and women into positions of great responsibility. But there is no continuing, orderly plan for the identification of capable young people and for their development. Their progress is frequently attributable to the unusual needs of new agencies established in each recurring emergency. Then the desperate need for additional executives, in both emergency and permanent agencies, pushes younger people up from the ranks with attention-attracting rapidity. Often their advancement, since it is founded on the needs of an emergency agency rather than of their own developed capabilities, is short-lived. When the emergency agency expires the individual is cast adrift with resultant loss to himself and the government.

PRINCIPLES ESSENTIAL TO A CAREER IN PUBLIC MANAGEMENT

The development of a career system necessitates the consideration of two principles new to the Federal personnel service. The first is that potential executives should be identified with the whole government rather than with a particular department. The individual's development should involve a variety of experiences in more than a single agency of the government. The development of such a government-wide service implies an effectiveness and influence on the part of the central personnel agency of the Federal government which the Civil Service Commission does not possess. Yet acceptance of this principle of government-wide service is essential if each individual entering the service is to be assured the maximum opportunity and if the Federal government is to have a pool of broadly experienced executives.

The second principle essential to the establishment of a career service in the management aspects of the Federal service is that the status or rank held by the individual should determine his compensation rather than the classification of the position held. This would mean that the individual who demonstrated especial accomplishment over a period of years would progress from rank to rank even though at a particular moment there might not be a position available at a higher classification level to which he might be assigned. This would mean, too, that those individuals who in times of emergency were sought for transfer to emergency agencies would retain their rank and compensation even though at the termination of the emergency there might be no immediately available position to which they could be assigned. Acceptance of this principle implies that in an enterprise as large as the Federal government it is inconceivable that the members of a limited corps of executives could not be usefully employed, even in periods of retrenchment and reorganization.

VIII. A POOL OF CAREER ADMINISTRATORS

THIS review of the current executive crisis argues strongly for the creation of a pool of career administrators.[1] The creation of such a pool would reduce the recurring necessity of borrowing individuals temporarily from business, universities, or labor organizations. It would make possible the use of those individuals who are borrowed and of officials who serve without compensation in positions where they can contribute their knowledge of the business system without being vulnerable to criticism for furthering their personal interests.

Note the term "pool." It is used designedly. It distinguishes the concept that is proposed here from the concepts of a career upon which the "Foreign Service," the "U.S. Public Health Service," and the British "administrative class" are founded. The terms "corps,"

[1] For similar proposals, more narrowly limited to individuals within the Federal civil service and perhaps the state services, see Leonard White, *Government Career Service* (University of Chicago Press, 1935), and an unpublished study by Lucius Wilmerding, Jr., prepared for the President's Committee on Civil Service Improvement, 1939.

"service," and "class" are abandoned for the less appealing term "pool."

What is needed is the identification and development of a number of trained individuals without the accompanying disadvantages of a "closed" corps. The existing "career corps" within the Federal government undoubtedly have advantages in attracting able recruits and endowing the members with prestige. Yet they each tend to become a closed caste, arrogating unto itself an increasing number of positions and fostering the entrenchment of its members in positions of power and influence.

With the exception of a few "career corps" which include a minority of all American public employees, this country's public service has never constituted a "sealed-off bureaucracy." Rather the Federal service has been characterized by an openness to public review and a high degree of accountability. This characteristic has been accompanied by (and has influenced) a fluid interchange of personnel between the Federal government, private business, and the state and local governments. This fluidity is attributable in part to the dynamic evolution of the Federal government. The addition of new functions has demanded the recruitment of new competences even while individuals experienced in governmental operations were required. These characteristics of constant review, accountability and fluidity have tended to keep the Federal civil servants alert and progressive and to prevent the development of an inflexible, castelike body of administrative officials.

The proposed "pool of career administrators" is conceived of as a fluid group of especially qualified men and women. The essential characteristics of this pool would be:

a) The identification of individuals throughout the Federal government possessing especial administrative competence and potential executive skill;
b) A regular program of transferring these individuals among Federal agencies in order to develop the individuals and establish a mobile group of experienced administrators;
c) The provision of a full measure of economic security for these members of the pool who continuingly demonstrate their competence;
d) A planned program of development, promotion, and rigorous appraisal for each member of the pool;
e) The endowment of these individuals with a recognition of competence and a public prestige that will enhance their effectiveness and their satisfaction with public employment.

The adoption of the two principles previously proposed would create a marked deviation from the existing practices and methods of the Federal civil service. Their adoption would run counter to the views of those who regard the Federal civil service (consciously or unconsciously) as designed exclusively to minimize political favoritism and to prevent discrimination against individuals in any minority group. But the adoption of these principles, as part of the important effort to create a pool of career administrators, is essential if the Federal civil service is to obtain and then retain a proportionate share of the nation's annual crop of able young people. These individuals will be attracted and held only if there is some guarantee that their abilities will be recognized, that they can look forward to progress commensurate with their demonstration of ability and, eventually, to a position which, if it does not offer compensation comparable to that enjoyed by others outside the government with like responsibilities, does offer prestige, respect, and broadening experience.

This proposed pool would be designed to provide a constant supply of trained executives. It would be made up only of individuals capable of being developed as top-level executives. Its members might have specialized in personnel management, budgeting, organization or methods work, or in other fields of management. But the acceptance of the individual into the pool should reflect the identification of the individual as one competent to perform as a "generalist" rather than a specialist.[2] The essential steps toward the creation of such a pool are agreement upon (a) the methods by which entrants will be selected; (b) the manner in which members of the pool will be developed for advancement; and (c) the assignment and utilization of the pool.

The Federal civil service examinations will bring in an

[2] Martin Friedman, assistant to Donald Dawson, Administrative Assistant to the President, speaking before the American Society for Public Administration on March 10, 1951, declared that a frequent difficulty in selecting career employees for top-level jobs in the Federal service was the location of individuals interested in and capable of dealing with program matters as distinguished from "housekeeping" affairs. Too many career civil servants are content, he declared, to serve as the "upstairs maid" to the executive rather than being willing to undertake operating responsibilities themselves.

adequate supply of capable people at the bottom—if there is the assurance of a respected, reasonably well compensated and progressive future, and if this assurance is aggressively advertised to this country's young people. From among those who have embarked on a career in the Federal service and have served with some measure of distinction for not less than three years, there should be a rigorous selection of those who should be admitted into the pool of administrators. The methods and criteria of selection should receive extended consideration. They should be designed to appraise not only the individual's education and work but also those extracurricular activities which suggest the breadth of the individual's intellectual curiosity of his potentialities for leadership.

The pool should be open to (a) employees within the Federal service—regardless of whether they entered the service in a manual, clerical, custodial, or professional position—who have achieved a position classified at Grade GS-10 and have not passed their thirtieth birthday; (b) to state and municipal civil service employees regardless of age who qualify for entry by such examinations and other criteria as may be established; and (c) to individuals from outside the public service who demonstrate, by such examinations and a record of accomplishment, their ability to perform effectively at any level in the Federal service.

Even more important would be the processes established for the development and periodic appraisal of those accepted into the pool. Membership in the pool should mean that the individual participates constantly in a carefully developed plan for professional development. This plan would include, especially in the early years of membership, regularly scheduled in-service training. But it should also include participation in the affairs of such professional associations as the American Society for Public Administration, the Society for the Advancement of Management, the American Management Association, and others. It might include periodic assignments for university training, such as the "short courses" for executive training at the Harvard School of Business Administration. It should include the encouragement of each individual to engage in extracurricular inquiry and to write for professional journals. It might include, too, periodic assignment of the individual to business enterprises for observation, experience, and training, and the provision of sabbatical leaves for more extended experience, observation, study, or travel. And it should inevitably include the regular, periodic appraisal of the services and prospects for further growth of each member of the pool.

The United States Civil Service Commission should select members of the pool, develop them, appraise them, and probably assign them. The Commission would have to permit the Federal departments to utilize members of the pool with considerable freedom and to retain them for extended periods. But the Commission would have to insure that each member of the pool was assigned to a variety of Federal agencies as a means of broadening his experience—and to identify him with the pool rather than with a particular bureau or department. Finally, the

Commission should insure that each successive assignment contributed, in so far as possible, to the development of the individual as a general executive rather than as a specialist.

The Commission would have to be especially mindful of the responsibilities related to the assignment and reassignment of members of the pool. It should discourage any tendency to perpetuate pool members in individual jobs or to identify jobs as available only to members of the pool. The pool should contribute to the more efficient conduct of the public business. It is not created to further the advancement of its members, even though that may be a by-product. Hence, to stave off the clique and caste characteristics of other career systems, every effort must be made to keep the pool flexible and open.

The prestige attached to membership in the pool would inevitably be related to the standards established for selection of entrants, to the success of plans for the development, training, and broadening of experience of each member of the pool, and to the character of the positions to which members of the pool are assigned. It would take time to establish this prestige in the minds of Federal department heads as well as in the public. Its establishment, however, is essential and should be an objective by which each step toward the establishment of the pool is measured.

The establishment of a government-wide pool of competent administrators is not a new idea. This recommendation is simply an adaptation of the most desirable characteristics of the British civil service and of practices found successful in a number of the larger American industrial enterprises. Here it is possible only to sketch in broad outlines the nature of this proposal. The numbers to be included within such a pool and the more detailed plans for the selection, development, and assignment of members deserve more thorough consideration than can be given in the compass of this inquiry.

A COMPLEMENTARY RESERVE

As a complement to this pool, the Federal government should explore the possibilities of creating a "public service reserve." The purpose of this reserve would be to identify a body of men and women with especial competences or familiarity with the business enterprise system and with a sufficient experience in public employment to make them immediately useful when their services are called for.

This reserve might be composed of individuals recruited from three sources. First, means should be developed to reserve the right to recall to the Federal service individuals who serve (and develop especial understanding and skills) during periods of emergency. Second, from each year's college and university graduates a number of individuals who are entering industry with especial promise might well be recruited into the "public service reserve" to be trained on a part-time basis in the processes of government, and to serve (even as National Guard members do) two weeks or a month each year in a Federal agency. Third, an additional number might well be trained each year in the U.S. Military Academy and in the U.S. Naval Academy with the idea that they would enter private business activities related to those functions which the military services must rapidly expand in times of emergency; for example, some of these graduates might be employed in the purchasing departments of industrial corporations or in the large railroad systems where they would progress as any other employee, but simultaneously they would be a member of the reserve, carry on part-time training, and periodically serve for a brief orientation period in one of the military departments.

This concept of a "public service reserve" has been advanced by several observers of the Federal government's need.[3] The concept has never been adequately explored. It offers the possibility of providing a variety of competence needed in the Federal government in times of emergency—but not continually—and of providing a method for more orderly and rapid expansion of the Federal government when that becomes necessary.

[3] The author bases this concept on suggestions advanced by Dr. J. Douglas Brown of Princeton University and Secretary of the Army Frank Pace. An earlier proposal for a United States Civil Service Reserve was made by Herbert Emmerich in "The Search for Executive Talent," a paper included in *Civil Service in Wartime*, edited by Leonard D. White (University of Chicago Press, 1945).

IX. THE NEED FOR THOROUGH INQUIRY

THERE is urgent need for more extended consideration of ways and means of meeting the basic problem—that is, how to insure an adequate supply of executive man-power for this country's most important, expanding enterprise. What we need is

a) A fuller awareness that a larger supply of executives and potential executives are urgently needed by the Federal government;
b) A larger share of the ablest young people among each year's college graduates, for service in the Federal government;
c) Greater salary and other incentives to retain and develop capable people within the Federal service;
d) A pool of career administrators and a complementary "public service reserve" to provide a mobile and expansible supply of qualified executive talent.

The citizenry of this country has been told and retold of the growth of government in terms of employees, of dollar expenditures, and of the cost in taxes. It has been warned of the "threatening drift toward Socialism." It has had the evolution of government in Britain pointed out as a hard example of the extremes toward which our government may be heading. And the citizenry of this country has been confronted during recent years with the realization that the threat of Russian domination and of the Communist philosophy places still additional responsibilities upon government—and costs upon the taxpayer.

But have these forces been interpreted in terms of the positive and peculiar role that has developed upon the Federal government—and in terms of the need for competent personnel? Government has not only expanded, but it has been forced into new functions and new processes by international, economic, and technological developments. During recent years many new institutions and processes of government have been developed. Some are in sharp contrast with traditional patterns. These include the government corporation and the practice of "contracting out," which has been used frequently by the Defense Department and by the Atomic Energy Commission. Moreover, in contrast with other governments, there is evidence that here we have extended government controls rather than attempting to nationalize enterprise.[1] Thus the Federal government may be work-

[1] For example, *The Economist*, January 6, 1951, p. 34, offered an illustration of the differing relationships between government and business in the then socialist state of Great Britain and in the United States. "Yearly financial accounts, in the form required by the Securities Exchange Commission, provide far more copious information than is customary in Britain. . . . American industry's attitude towards

ing out a balance between governmental control and private enterprise, which means much to the evolution of the capitalistic free enterprise system as well as to the character and numbers of individuals who shall serve their government in the future.

For the more extended consideration that is proposed it is essential first that we provide an imaginative conception of the role of the Federal government a generation hence. With that conception in mind, the consideration must focus upon the prospective, aggregate need for executive talent and upon the assortment of skills that will be needed in executive positions to provide the variety of services required by a democratic government concerned with the maintenance of a healthy, vigorous free-enterprise system. Especial effort should be made to "spell out" the responsibilities peculiar to the environment of the executive in the public service, so that we may think more clearly about the qualities of mind and temperament required of the public executive. Attention should be given to those factors which have caused the low esteem in which the public service is held. Inevitably, in the course of this consideration, one will have to explore the attitude of members of Congress to-

---

what some corners of British industry denounce as "formfilling" is typified by one instance: twice when the Department of Commerce's appropriations were reduced and it had to curtail the collection of figures for business statistical series, industry through its trade associations paid the Government to continue the service. Five Government bureaux collect business data, as do some 400 of the 1,400 American trade associations and several private and semi-public bodies—yet 'industry is prepared to support in every way the compilation of figures' (and is also consulted about their form and collection far more than is British business)."

ward the basic problems involved, and the manner in which the separation of legislative and executive powers adds to the responsibilities of a Federal executive, and the skills that he needs.

This frame of reference will emphasize the expanding role and evolving character of government in a civilization where an increasing proportion of the population lives in large cities and works as employees as well as the necessity of limiting the burden and impact of government through taxes and controls on the millions of business enterprises which contribute to the welfare of the society. Recognition of the nature of the government required by this frame of reference will reveal not only the human resources required but the essentiality of public understanding. Every medium of communication must be used to help the American people translate our unstable economy, the "Garrison State," and the role of the United States in world affairs into an understanding of the responsibilities of government.

On several important public questions during the past few decades real advances have been made as the result of thorough studies, some of them by commissions of inquiry under public or private auspices, others by individual observers. Studies of this kind have simultaneously focused public attention on and developed new understanding of such problems as the freedom of the press, the needs of our public schools, and the nature of medical education. They have not always attracted widespread interest or mass support. But they have mobilized the interests of those few leaders capable of stimulating effective action. In the past one privately financed commission (the Commission of Inquiry on Public Service Personnel) and several publicly supported ones have delved into the problem of manpower for government. But no comprehensive consideration has been given to this problem for approximately two decades. It is high time, hence, that an effort be made to explore the problem, devise remedies, and simultaneously prod the thoughtful leaders in a few communities to aid in coping with the problem.

If, in addition, genuine public understanding of the urgency of this need can be achieved, then it will assuredly be possible to gain support for those measures which will facilitate the assembly in the Federal government of an experienced, knowledgeable, and versatile corps of individuals competent to plan and manage the increasing variety of activities entrusted to government. Such human resources constitute an essential ingredient of the further development of American civilization.

DATE DUE

OCT 18 1978			
			PRINTED IN U.S.A.